Mountains

KINGFISHER

a Houghton Mifflin Company imprint
222 Berkeley Street
Boston, Massachusetts 02116
www.houghtonmifflinbooks.com

First published in 2007
2 4 6 8 10 9 7 5 3 1

1TR/1106/PROSP/RNB/140MA/F

LIBRARY OF CONGRESS CATALOGING-IN-PUBLICATION DATA
Hynes, Margaret, 1970–
Mountains/Margaret Hynes.—1st ed.
p. cm. — (Kingfisher young knowledge)
1. Mountains—Juvenile literature. I. Title.
GB512.H96 2007
551.43'2—dc22
2006022388

ISBN-13: 978-0-7534-6037-5

Senior editor: Belinda Weber
Coordinating editor: Caitlin Doyle
Designer: Rebecca Johns
Cover designer: Poppy Jenkins
Picture research manager: Cee Weston-Baker
DTP coordinator: Catherine Hibbert
DTP operator: Claire Cessford
Production controller: Jessamy Oldfield
Indexer: Hilary Bird

Printed in China

Acknowledgments
The publishers would like to thank the following for permission to reproduce their material. Every care has been taken
to trace copyright holders. However, if there have been unintentional omissions or failure to trace copyright holders,
we apologize and will, if informed, endeavor to make corrections in any future edition.
b = bottom, c = center, l = left, t = top, r = right

Photographs: cover Getty Stone; 1 Corbis/W. Wayne Lockwood; 2–3 Corbis/Charlie Munsey; 4–5 Alamy/Nagelestock; 6–7 Corbis/Eye
Ubiquitous; 7tr Corbis/Galen Rowell; 9 Corbis/Reuters; 10–11 Photolibrary.com; 11br Getty/Science Faction; 12 Corbis/Joseph Sohm;
13 Corbis/Ric Ergenbright; 15tr Frank Lane Picture Agency/Winfried Wisniewski; 15bl Arboretum de Villardebelle, France; 16–17 Getty/
Stone; 17br Alamy/Aflo Foto; 18l Corbis/Galen Rowell; 18–19 Getty/Imagebank; 19r Photolibrary.com; 20 Corbis/Eye Ubiquitous;
21t Corbis/Tom Bean; 21br Corbis/Paul A. Souders; 22 Alamy/Brett Baunton; 23t Natural History Picture Agency/Alberto Nardi;
23b Science Photo Library/Kaj R. Svensson; 24 Corbis/Steve Kaufman; 25t Alamy/Imagina Photography; 25b Corbis/Joe McDonald;
26c Alamy/Andrew Woodley; 26–27b Getty/Stone; 27t Alamy/Terry Fincher Photos; 28–29 Photolibrary.com; 29t Alamy/Mediacolor's;
30 Corbis/Zefa; 31t Getty/Photographer's Choice; 31br Getty/Aurora; 32 Getty/Digital Vision; 33tl Alamy/David R. Frazier Photolibrary;
33b Alamy/Phototake; 34 Alamy/Publiphoto Diffusion; 35tl John Cleare Mountain Camera; 35b Getty/Photographer's Choice;
36c Royal Geographical Society; 36br Corbis Montagne Magazine; 37 Corbis/Sygma; 38 Alamy/f1 online; 38–39 Alamy/StockShot;
39c Corbis/Ashley Cooper; 40 Corbis/EPA; 41t Corbis/John van Hasselt; 41b Frank Lane Picture Agency/Foto Natura;
43tl Getty/NGS; 43b Mary Evans Picture Library; 48 Alamy/Imagestate

Illustrations on pages: 8, 11, 12, 13, 16 Peter Winfield; 14–15 Steve Weston
Commissioned photography on pages 44–47 by Andy Crawford
Project maker and photo shoot coordinator: Jane Thomas
Thank you to models Jamie Chang-Leng, Mary Conquest, and Georgina Page

KFYK Kingfisher Young Knowledge

Mountains

Margaret Hynes

KINGFISHER
BOSTON

Contents

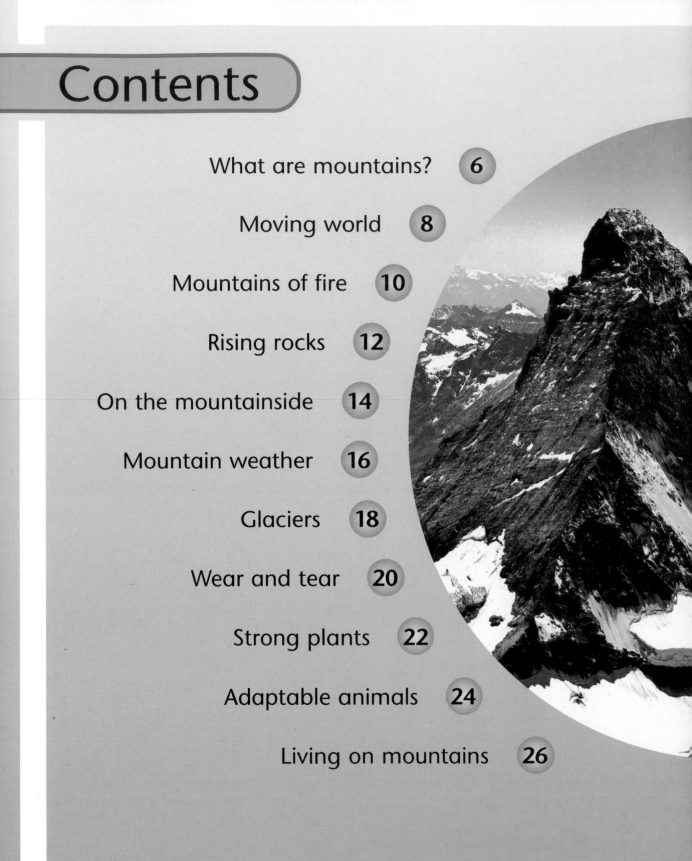

What are mountains?

A mountain is a giant rock with steep sides that rises above Earth's surface. There are mountains on land, under the oceans, and even on other planets.

Mighty mountain ranges

A group of mountains is called a range. The Himalayas is a mountain range in Asia. It is the home of the world's highest peaks.

peaks—the top parts of a mountain

Cold at the top

There is less, or "thinner," air at the top of a mountain than there is at the bottom. It is also colder, so some peaks are snowy all year round.

air—the mixture of gases we breathe

Moving world

Earth's rocky surface is called the crust. It is divided into plates, which fit together like a jigsaw puzzle. The plates move very slowly over the face of the planet.

Moving plates

This map shows the plates and the direction that they are moving in. Some plates crash into each other, while others pull apart.

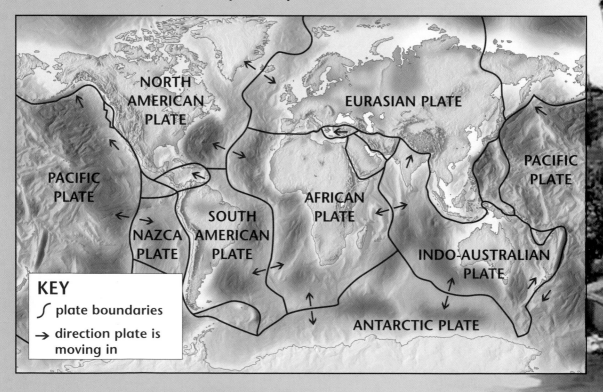

NORTH AMERICAN PLATE

EURASIAN PLATE

PACIFIC PLATE

PACIFIC PLATE

AFRICAN PLATE

SOUTH AMERICAN PLATE

NAZCA PLATE

INDO-AUSTRALIAN PLATE

ANTARCTIC PLATE

KEY
ʃ plate boundaries
→ direction plate is moving in

plates—large areas of land that "float" on top of the liquid rock underneath

Earthquakes

When the edges of two plates grip each other, the plates cannot move. If they shift suddenly, an earthquake happens, causing terrible damage.

crust—*the hard, rocky surface of Earth*

Mountains of fire

Some mountains are volcanoes. They form when hot, melted rock, called magma, erupts from a crack in Earth's crust. The liquid rock cools down and hardens into a mountain.

Violent eruption

Mount Etna is a volcano in Italy. When it erupts, magma bursts out. Ash, gas, steam, and hot rocks shoot up into the sky.

erupts—explodes, throwing ash, gas, and hot rocks up into the air

Hot spots

The Hawaiian islands are volcanoes. They form as the Pacific plate passes over a hot and active area called a hot spot.

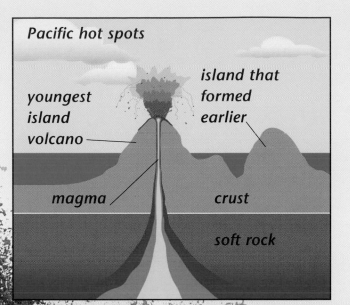

Pacific hot spots

youngest island volcano

island that formed earlier

magma

crust

soft rock

Flowing lava

Once magma pours out of a volcano it is called lava. It rolls downhill, like a river of fire.

lava—melted rock on Earth's surface

Rising rocks

Many mountains form in areas where plates push against each other. The moving plates squeeze the land upward, creating mountains.

squeezing action pushes up blocks of rock

Fault-block mountains

The moving plates can cause cracks in the crust. These break the crust into blocks, and some rise up to form fault-block mountains.

continent A

continent B

Rounded off

The Wasatch Range in Utah is a fault-block mountain range. Its blocky shape has been worn down over time.

fault—*a crack in Earth's crust*

Fold mountains

When two plates crash together, they can cause layers of rock in the crust to buckle and rise. This forms fold mountains.

valley

mountain

continent A crashes into continent B

continent B

Folding rock

As the layers of rock in the crust are squashed, they form zigzagging shapes called folds.

buckle—*to crumple and fold*

On the mountainside

A high mountain has several zones, or regions. Each zone has different plants and animals. Very few plants or animals live close to the top.

conifers

Plant cover

Forests cover the mountain's lower region. Farther up is a zone of small, low-lying plants called alpines.

deciduous trees

conifers—*evergreen trees that keep their leaves all year round*

icy peak

alpine
region

Mountain birds

The wind is so strong at the top of mountains that only powerful birds, such as this lammergeier, can fly there.

Conifers

These cones and pine needles belong to the spruce conifer. Conifer trees have a triangular shape. This helps the snow slide off them.

deciduous trees—trees that lose their leaves in the fall

Mountain weather

The weather can change very quickly on mountains. A storm can start in just a few minutes. The temperature can quickly drop to below freezing.

Rain shelter

Some mountains are so high that they block rain clouds. One slope may be rainy, while the other side stays dry.

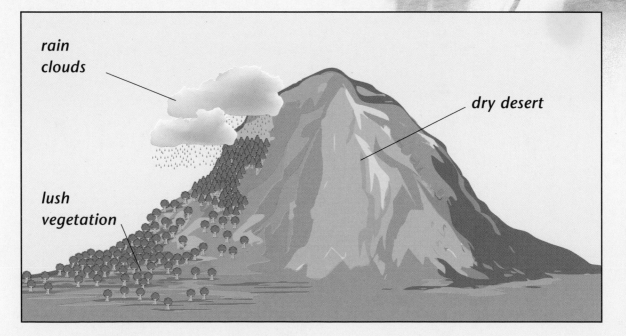

rain clouds

dry desert

lush vegetation

vegetation—plant life

Blizzards

Howling winds whip up mountain snow into storms called blizzards. These make climbing much more difficult.

Burning sun

Sunlight passes through the thin mountain air easily. Snow reflects the rays of light onto skin and can cause sunburn, even when it is cold.

reflects—*when light rays bounce back from the surface*

Glaciers

Giant rivers of ice, called glaciers, form on the peaks of some of the world's highest mountains. The glaciers move downhill very slowly.

How glaciers form

Snow collects in rocky hollows, called cirques, high up on the mountain. The snow turns into ice and forms a glacier.

hollows—shallow holes

Cracks in the ice

Cracks called crevasses form in a glacier as it moves over bumpy ground. They are very deep and dangerous, so climbers use safety ropes.

Left behind

Glaciers pick up rubble and drag it along with them. When the ice melts, these rocks are left behind.

rubble—a mixture of stones and rocks of different sizes

Wear and tear

All mountains are under attack from the elements. Ice, wind, and running water slowly wear them down over millions of years.

Old mountain

A young mountain is jagged. As it gets older, the elements slowly wear it down, and it becomes more rounded.

elements—the group name for earth, fire, air, and water

Ice sculptures

As a glacier creeps along,
it scrapes at the mountainside.
Eventually it gouges out huge
U-shaped valleys such as this
one in California.

Rolling rocks

Ice chisels away small
rocks from the mountain.
These tumble down the
slope and collect in
a pile at the bottom.

jagged—has a sharp, uneven surface and outline

Strong plants

Plants that grow high up on the mountain slopes have adapted to cope with the bitter cold, fierce winds, and freezing weather that are found there.

Tiny trees

Some willow and birch trees grow high up on the mountainside. They avoid the howling winds by hugging the ground.

acids—substances that can eat away other substances

Alpine snowbell

The alpine snowbell gives off heat, which melts the snow around it. The plant's heat enables it to bloom in the spring.

Growing on rocks

Lichens live on rocky peaks. They make acids that cause the rocks to crumble. Then they send tiny roots into the rocks to suck up any nutrients in them.

adapted—changed over time

Adaptable animals

Some animals that live on mountains have adapted in order to live on the steep slopes. Others have adapted to living with high winds and freezing conditions.

Hot bath

Japanese macaque monkeys wallow in hot pools during the cold winters. The water is heated by volcanoes.

Mountain climber

Mountain goats are good at climbing over the rocky mountain faces. Their hooves are hollow and act like suction cups, helping the goats grip the surface.

Natural antifreeze

The Yarrow's spiny lizard's blood stays liquid in temperatures below freezing, which allows it to survive on icy peaks in Mexico.

antifreeze—a substance that prevents things from freezing

Living on mountains

Mountain peoples have learned to live in steep, remote, and sometimes dangerous places. They grow crops for food and raise animals there.

Mountain animals

Yaks are useful animals. They provide food and wool to farmers. They are also used to carry goods.

Mountain cities

The city of Kathmandu is nestled in the Himalayas. It has the same facilities as any other modern city.

Growing food

Mountain fields are steep, and there is not much soil. Many farmers build terraces to stop the soil from washing away.

terraces—steplike fields

Going places

It can be difficult to travel on mountains because they are very steep. People have come up with useful ways for making travel on mountains easier.

Long and winding roads

Mountain roads do not follow a straight line because they would be too steep to climb. The roads take a zigzagging route instead.

zigzagging—*twisting and turning*

Climbing on a cable

A moving cable pulls this cable car between stations at the top and bottom of a mountain. Skiers use cable cars to get to snow that is high up on mountains.

cable—a long, thick rope, usually made from metal wire

Tourism

Mountains are great places to explore and enjoy. People can ski, trek, climb, or mountain bike along the steep slopes. But we must protect these places so that everyone can enjoy them in the future.

Jumping off

Hang gliders jump off mountaintops to float down on their wings. They glide on the warm air that rises up from the ground.

protect—to take care of something and keep it away from harm

Winter sports

Skiers and snowboarders love snow-covered mountains. They can slide and jump down the slippery slopes.

When the snow melts

Many tourists drop their garbage on mountains when they visit. This pollutes the area and can harm the wildlife that lives there.

pollutes—*makes harmful waste that damages the environment*

Mountain resources

Hidden inside of mountains are valuable resources such as building materials and metals. There are also useful resources on the slopes such as trees.

Building blocks

Each day big dump trucks remove tons of rocks and rubble from mountains. This is used to make buildings and bridges.

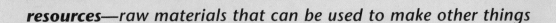

resources—*raw materials that can be used to make other things*

Cutting down trees

Logging companies plant fast-growing trees on mountainsides. When the trees are grown, loggers cut them down to use as timber and fuel.

Mining metal

Some mountain rocks are rich in gold, silver, copper, and tin. Miners use large drills to dig these metals out of the stone.

fuel—*a substance that is used for producing heat or power by burning*

Mountaineering today

Today's mountaineers are very prepared for their climbs. They have special food for energy, layers of clothing for warmth, and lots of safety equipment.

A good night's rest

Mountaineers shelter in tents at night and during bad weather. The tents are light to carry, strong, and waterproof.

safety equipment—ropes, harnesses, and picks that are needed for climbing

Oxygen supply

Climbers carry tanks of oxygen, which they use to help them breathe more easily in the thin mountain air.

Climbing suit

Climbers wear one-piece suits that are filled with down for warmth. The suit is windproof and waterproof.

down—soft, hairlike feathers that cover young birds

Reaching the top

Mountain climbing is a popular sport. Many people have now climbed some of the highest mountains, including the tallest mountain on land, Mount Everest.

George Mallory

Andrew Irvine

Last climb

Mallory and Irvine began to climb Mount Everest in 1924. Both men died on the mountain, but no one knows if they reached the top before they died.

Extraordinary climber

Reinhold Messner has climbed the world's 14 highest peaks. He is the first person to climb Mount Everest without extra oxygen.

oxygen—*one of the gases in air*

Wonder woman

Catherine Destivelle is a world-class climber. She often tackles dangerous slopes and often only uses one or two of her fingers to pull herself up.

world-class—*some of the best in the world*

Avalanche!

A large mass of snow and ice can suddenly break loose and crash down a mountainside. This is called an avalanche.

Predicting avalanches

Scientists use the information that they gather in weather stations like this one to help them predict when avalanches are likely to happen.

predicting—knowing that something is going to happen

Avalanche in action

Some avalanches move as fast as a race car. They sweep away everything in their path, including trees, people, and even villages.

Protection

This steel fence has been built to stop an avalanche from reaching the town farther downhill. It will slow down an avalanche.

steel—*a strong metal made from iron and carbon*

Mountain rescue

Even experienced mountaineers can get into trouble on mountains. When they do, well-equipped and specially trained teams are ready to race to the rescue.

Sliding stretcher
Rescuers sometimes use special sliding stretchers to glide the injured person down the mountainside.

experienced—*people who have skills that they have gained over time*

Helicopter rescue

Helicopters can reach remote peaks quickly. Rescuers can then help the injured people and take them to a hospital.

Rescue dog

Saint Bernard dogs have a strong sense of smell. They can be specially trained to sniff out the victims of avalanches.

remote—out of the way places

Mountain mysteries

People sometimes see some strange things when they climb a mountain. They might find fossilized fish, or they might be followed by a huge shadow.

Ghostly shadow

If someone climbs a mountain when the sun is low, the sun casts an enormous shadow on any low clouds.

fossil—the remains of ancient animals or plants that are found in rocks

Something fishy

People often find fossilized fish in rocks in fold mountains. Millions of years ago these mountains were part of the seabed.

Bigfoot

Some people believe that a large creature called Bigfoot roams around the Rocky Mountains. No one knows if it really exists.

seabed—the land at the bottom of the sea

Making mountains

Make a fold mountain range

Discover how land is forced upward when two plates collide by doing this simple experiment.

1

Roll out each ball of clay to make a rough square that is one inch thick.

You will need
- 2 balls of modeling clay in different colors
- Tray
- Rolling pin
- Plastic wrap

2

Lay both pieces on the plastic wrap on the tray 0.5 in. apart.

Gently push the two clay blocks together. Your mountain range will rise upward.

Leaving footprints

Bigfoot's calling card

Bigfoot's footprints are called its "calling card." Make one to give to a friend.

You will need
- Large sheet of cardboard
- Paints and paintbrush
- Marker or felt-tip pen
- Scissors
- Sponge

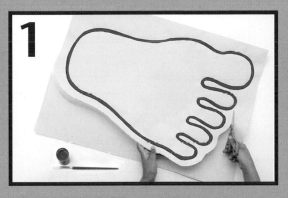

1 Fold the cardboard in half, then paint a big foot shape. Cut out the shape, but do not cut the folded side.

2 On a sponge, draw a smaller foot shape. Cut this out.

3 Dip the sponge in some paint and decorate your card with lots of little footprints walking up toward the toes.

Your giant calling card is ready. Write a message inside.

Moving cable car

Make a cable car

Cable cars can climb up high mountains on moving cables. Make a model with stations at the top and bottom of your mountain range.

You will need

- 3 small cereal boxes
- Colored paper
- Sharp colored pencil
- Modeling clay
- 1 long, 1 short piece of string
- Marbles
- Tape
- 1 small candy box

1

Cover the cereal boxes with colored paper. Decorate it with shapes of mountains and trees.

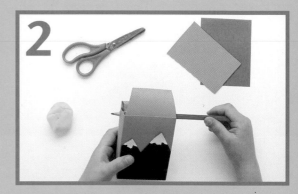

2

Pierce a hole in the top of each box with a sharp pencil. Use modeling clay to push against.

3

Thread the long piece of string through the holes, as shown.

4

Place some marbles in each box, then tape the boxes closed.

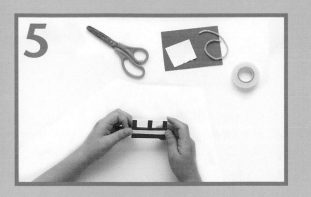

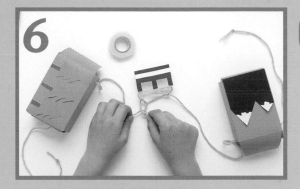

Decorate the small candy box with colored paper to make it look like a cable car.

Tape the short piece of string to the car, then tie it to the middle of the long piece of string.

Index